LITTLE PINK BOOK™

When Your Teacher
Has Cancer

Helping Children Cope in the Classroom and Beyond

Maryann Makekau

20/30north Studios

Other Little Pink Book™ titles available soon:
When Your Mom Has Cancer – Helping Children Cope at Home and Beyond
When Your Grandma Has Cancer – Helping Children Cope at Home and Beyond
When Your Sister Has Cancer – What to Expect and How to Help
When Your Friend Has Cancer – What to Expect and How to Help
When Your Husband Walks Beside You and Cancer – Helping Families Cope

1

For information, address:
Maryann Makekau
PO Box 2021
Fort Walton Beach, FL 32549
author@thelittlepinkbooks.com

Set in Kristen ITC 12 point font. Includes references.

Library of Congress Cataloging (Pre-assigned Control Number)
Makekau, Maryann
LITTLE PINK BOOK™ - When Your Teacher Has Cancer: Helping Children Cope in the Classroom and Beyond

ISBN-13:978-0-61532-828-7
ISBN-10:0-61532-828-8

Note: The information in this book is true and complete to the best of our knowledge. This book is intended only as an informative guide for those wishing to know more about cancer issues. In no way is this book intended to replace, countermand or conflict with the advice given to you by your own physician. The ultimate decision concerning care should be made between you and your doctor. We strongly recommend you follow his or her advice. Information in this book is general and is offered with no guarantees on the part of the author or publisher. The author and publisher disclaim all liability in connection with use of this book.

2

Foreword

Cancer is a sneak. It shows up uninvited, seeking to wreak havoc in bodies, families, schools and workplaces. It arrives unexpectedly and demands immediate attention at the expense of everything else. Cancer wants to have the last word, and sometimes it does — unless hope meets it head-on.

Hope enters the scene just in time. When fear strikes, hope says no. When uncertainty and confusion reign, hope is the light that brings peace, clarity and direction. Hope takes many forms. It is there when a friend offers to pray, cook, clean or babysit. It warms hearts in hugs, letters and thoughtful notes. It is heard in the word "remission" spoken by a doctor and fuels steadfastness through the stories of those who have persevered and conquered. Hope is also there as one learns what to expect if cancer shows up and, especially, all that can be done about it.

This Little Pink Book™ overflows with hope.

It is full of practical tips for those who want to understand, help and love those fighting cancer, particularly children whose teachers are facing this illness. It highlights the importance of telling children the truth about their teacher's cancer in an age-appropriate and helpful way.

Maryann Makekau writes in simple language that school children can grasp. The sweet and playful illustrations appeal to children, help them stay engaged despite a difficult topic, and help to facilitate discussions between child and parent or teacher. This book has a refreshing simplicity, creative suggestions and is clearly written by someone who understands the needs of those with cancer and the people who love them. From an illustration using soap bubbles to describe our cells to the suggestion that children draw themselves hugging their teacher, Maryann's book educates, refreshes, comforts and empowers both children and adults.

When I was in my late teens, I walked with my mother as she faced breast cancer. She changed before my eyes physically and in unexpected ways, yet I witnessed her remaining inwardly strong and joyful through the love, care and attention of her loved ones. My beautiful mother, Maribel, faced cancer with inspiring courage and grace, leaving me with the conviction that faith, hope and love can transform anything.

This Little Pink Book™ contains much of what I wish somebody had explained to me back then. I know that it will help many children and adults as they walk through a valley that, through hope, can become a living spring. May it be so for you.

Amaryllis Sánchez Wohlever, MD
Grace Medical Home
51 Pennsylvania Street
Orlando, FL 32806
www.gracemedicalhome.org

4

Gratitude

This book is dedicated to my teacher friend, Vicki. As she began the battle with breast cancer, she courageously continued to teach her 2nd graders, her "little ducklings." Explaining it to her ducklings was not an easy task during that time of loss. This Little Pink Book™ was created to provide extra help in comforting her students. It has since found its way into the hands of young and old, inside and outside the classroom – providing hope for patients and loved ones who are fighting the fight together. God bless my friend, Vicki, who is always an inspiration and source of strength.

Thank you to my friends and family who read this book many times over, providing their helpful comments, suggestions and enthusiasm. I especially want to thank my husband, Chuck, who gives of his time, love and patience so I can write. To my son, Derek at 2030north Studios, for his expertise in giving class to stick-characters, for playful illustrations and graphic layout, and especially his tireless efforts in helping me launch this book. Thank you to my daughter, Loren for sharpening my eyes for the hurting – God is always showing us new ways of using that gift.

Special thanks to Dr. Mari and Laurie, for dedicating their time and bilingual skills in creating the upcoming Spanish version of this book. To Pastor James: "when you see something missing, perhaps it is God telling you to fill the gap" – those words inspired me to create this book!

Profits are earmarked for nonprofit organizations which aid in awareness, diagnosis and treatment of breast cancer.

5

Table of Contents

What is Cancer?

Cancer is a sickness that can show up in different areas of the body – lungs, breast, liver, stomach, and other places.   This book is about teachers with breast cancer. Many people will not get cancer, but sometimes people we love do get it.

Your body still has lots of healthy parts even when a sickness is found. The cells in your body look kind of like tiny bubbles.

Remember blowing soap bubbles with a wand? You can watch them float up high into the air...until...they burst! Our body cells look a little like that under a micro-scope, but not so round and they don't burst like that.

Cancer is when healthy cells become damaged and then those cells go out and damage (or hurt) other cells.

Yet, healthy cells can still work together for good. Medicines and surgery can help clean up the damaged cells that caused the cancer.

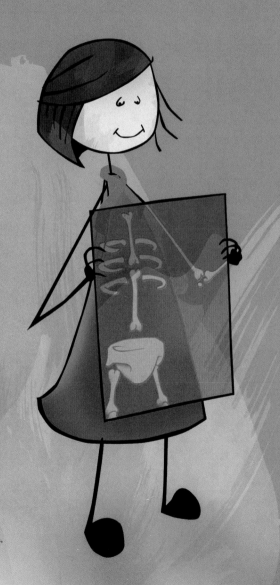

Surgery can mean the bad cells are removed or just some of them are looked at under a microscope, so that the doctors can see them better. It's hard to see what's inside our bodies without doing this. Have you ever tried to look through your stomach or see your lungs? But you know that they are there because God made them inside everyone's body!

Depending on the cancer and the treatment or medicines used, the cancer might last a short time or it might take longer to go away. You may have someone in your family who has had cancer; you may even know someone who died from cancer. People with cancer don't always die from it. In fact, many times doctors can find the cancer when it's just starting and they're able to make it all go away. Doctors call this "remission." Complete remission means that the cancer isn't there anymore, the sickness is all gone. When your teacher is all better, she will be back to teach you new things again!

IS IT CATCHY?

You might be wondering if you can get cancer from someone else, is it contagious (catchy)? The answer is NO. You can't get cancer that way, just like you can't get someone's hair color by being near them. Hugging someone with brown hair won't turn your blonde hair into brown hair, will it? It's sort of like that; you stay just the way you are, even when you hug someone with cancer. And if someone with cancer takes medicines that make their hair fall out, yours won't fall out too. You won't lose yours because they do!

Sometimes, while your teacher is going through

12

the healing time she won't be able to give hugs like she used to. It takes time to heal from surgery and it makes her body hurt for awhile. The medicines might make her very tired too. But you can save up all those hugs and give them to her when she's all better.

Maybe you want to keep score of "saved hugs." You can also draw a picture of a hug to give to your teacher. Even if you think that you're not good at drawing yet, stick-figured people are easy to draw and they look really awesome!

FEELINGS

Adults and children get all kinds of feelings when someone they love is sick. You may feel angry or sad. You may feel bad or afraid. You may feel confused or frustrated. You may feel all those things at different times. If you've ever moved to a new place or lost a pet,

happy   sad   angry

you understand some of those feelings. All those feelings are okay. You should talk to your mom or dad about those feelings and it's okay to tell your teacher too. Although your teacher is sad about having cancer, she is also very strong.

During sad times you may not be able to understand some things or say what you wish you could. Faith in God can help you feel stronger. You need to know that you can't make your teacher's cancer go away and you didn't do anything to make it happen either. It's even okay for

scared

frustrated

confused

you to still laugh and have fun! Your teacher appreciates your hard work in the classroom and she loves to see your smile and happy face.

MAKING CANCER GO AWAY

The doctor will try to make the cancer go away so that your teacher will not be sick anymore. It would be nice if we could just put it into a box and mail it somewhere else, but it doesn't work that way. Cancer only goes away with "treatment." Treatment means that a doctor may do surgery and give medicine. When you have a cold, your mother gives you medicines that make you feel better. Sometimes, the medicine doesn't taste good and you might even throw up! Cancer medicine might make your teacher sick like that for awhile, because it doesn't taste good to her body either.

But just like you have to take that cold medicine even though you don't like it, your teacher has to take her medicine.

16

17

The most common medicines for cancer are called "chemotherapy" and "radiation." Those are big words that mean to get rid of the cancer in the body. Sometimes, there are other medicines used instead of chemotherapy or radiation.

It can take awhile to get rid of the cancer, so your teacher will be absent. She will make sure that you have a really good substitute while she's gone and she will visit you as soon as she can. It is important that your teacher feels really strong before she comes back to teach you. Being sick makes you very tired. Taking care of yourself by resting makes you better faster.

Your teacher will smile

whenever she hears how hard you're working – she'll be asking about you even when you don't see her. You can draw pictures, make cards or write letters to her and give them to her when she returns. Make sure you do this only when your substitute teacher says your class work is finished though!

MY TEACHER LOOKS DIFFERENT

Have you ever dressed up in a costume? Wearing a costume can make you look really different. Especially if you wear fake hair on your head, that's called a wig! When someone is going through the treatment to get rid of cancer it sometimes changes the way they look. Their skin might become pale; they may look really tired and not smile as much as they used to. It doesn't mean that they're angry; it's just really hard work to get well. If your teacher needs the medicine called "chemotherapy" or "radiation treatment," it might make her hair fall out. But sometimes her hair won't fall out at all! It all depends on the treatment or medicine she has to take to get rid of the cancer.

Wigs come in different colors: brown, blonde, red – just like real hair! If your teacher loses her hair she'll get to wear lots of different wigs! Don't worry, her hair will grow back! Sometimes it grows back curly or straight, thick or thin – but it does grow back. This can be fun for your teacher because she can play dress up with all the wigs! So if she looks different to you don't be afraid, she's still the same teacher you've always known. And don't be afraid to ask questions. It is much better to really know the answer than just imagine it. If your teacher doesn't have the answer, she will do her best to get you one.

HELPING YOUR TEACHER
AND CLASSMATES

When someone you love is sick, it can make you feel confused and not sure about what to do. It can also make you feel sad because you can't fix it or make it go away. There are other things you can do that are helpful though.

You can write a book like this one! You can draw pictures! You can do all your work in the class-room and at home! You might even work harder on something that you need to improve! You can look for ways to be helpful to others! You can make others smile and laugh! You can help a classmate who is sad by giving a hug! You can share the ways you're helping with your family!

You can start wearing pink shirts, pink bracelets or pink shoelaces! Did you know that people who battle breast cancer and their families and friends often wear pink? They wear pink ribbons, pink bracelets, pink hats, pink shirts and more.

They do this to show that they want to bless people who have to fight breast cancer and also those who love them.   There are many ways to help your teacher and your class-mates. Not sure what to do?   Just ask your teacher!

23

PRE-TREATMENT TIPS FOR TEACHERS

1. Healing is as individual as the blueprint God used in creating you. Maintain realistic expectations for each day, even if it is different than yesterday or the days before that.

2. Remember to engage in something funny every day. Start collecting comic strips from the newspaper, a list of funny movies (Penguin movies do count!), and old photos that make you laugh. These will be your laughter stockpile – humor is one of God's best healing gifts.

3. Start hugging others until they let go – never let go first. This will be your storehouse during the times that hugging hurts and you just can't go there.

4. Write down your favorite 10 recipes to give to friends who are asking what they can do to help. They can use these recipes to bring meals to you and your family on treatment days. You will then know that everyone is taken care of and your husband can be with you instead of in the kitchen. And your friends will be blessed to help you!

5. Allow time to grieve. If you don't like to cry, set a timer for 15 minutes and cry your eyes out – then clean up and move forward. Do this as often as possible and necessary.

6. Have an electric blanket on hand, if permissible by the doctor. If you get chills or have trouble falling asleep, it is a warm welcome! A heavy quilt is a good substitute.

7. It's okay to get angry – God can take it! (p.s. Your family may need warning.)

8. Create a dream-sheet, write down what you've imagined but not accomplished. Give yourself something to look forward to when your body is restored.

9. Check-out for 15 minutes a day. Commune with God by just being still and imagining His great big arms around you, taking away your fears one by one.

10. Find one thing you absolutely love about yourself and write it on a post-it note. Put this where you will see it often so that when you "look different" in the midst of the battle, you can focus on what makes you special and unique and thank God for it.

11. Spend time outside each day enjoying some fresh air and the beauty of nature.

12. Read uplifting, inspiring, hope-filled books and move away from negative or fearful comments, books or people.

RESOURCES FOR TEACHERS AND PARENTS

Helpful Reads:
• What is Cancer Anyway? Explaining Cancer to Children of All Ages (coloring book) by Karen L. Carney
• Because Someone I Love Has Cancer: Kids Activity Book - The American Cancer Society
• The Paper Chain by Claire Blake, Eliza Blanchard and Kathy Parkison
• Just Get Me through This: A Practical Guide to Breast Cancer by Deborah Cohen and MD Robert M. Gelfand
• Choices in Breast Cancer Treatment: Medical Specialists and Cancer Survivors Tell You What You Need to Know by Kenneth D. Miller, MD
• Breast Cancer Husband: How to Help Your Wife (and Yourself) During Diagnosis, Treatment and Beyond by Marc Silver
• The Breast Cancer Survivor's Fitness Plan: A Doctor-Approved Workout Plan for a Strong Body and Lifesaving Results by Carolyn Kaelin, Francesca Coltrera, Jose Gardiner and Joy Prouty

Helpful Sites:
• www.bcrfcure.org
• www.nationalbreastcancer.org
• www.cancer.org
• www.cancer.gov
• www.beliefnet.com (search breast cancer articles)
• www.motherslivingstories.org

The power of prayer:
Rely on friends and family as your warriors for healing.

References used for this publication:
• www.nationalbreastcancer.org
• www.komen.org
• www.cancer.org

26

QUESTIONS

NOTES

28

Made in the USA
Middletown, DE
15 August 2019